For Nancy
of the Swanton tribe!

Bill Everson
Santa Cruz

by William Everson

VERSE

These Are the Ravens (1935)
San Joaquin (1939)
The Masculine Dead (1942)
The Waldport Poems (1944)
War Elegies (1944)
The Residual Years (1944)
Poems MCMXLII (1945)
The Residual Years (1948)
A Privacy of Speech (1949)
Triptych for the Living (1951)
An Age Insurgent (1959)
The Crooked Lines of God (1959)
The Year's Declension (1961)
The Hazards of Holiness (1962)
The Poet is Dead (1964)
The Blowing of the Seed (1966)
Single Source (1966)
The Rose of Solitude (1967)
In the Fictive Wish (1967)
A Canticle to the Waterbirds (1968)
The Springing of the Blade (1968)
The Residual Years (1968)
The City Does not Die (1969)
The Last Crusade (1969)
Who Is She that Looketh Forth as the Morning (1972)
Tendril in the Mesh (1973)
Black Hills (1973)
Man-Fate (1974)
River-Root/A Syzygy (1976)
The Mate-Flight of Eagles (1977)
Rattlesnake August (1978)
The Veritable Years (1978)
The Masks of Drought (1980)

PROSE

Robinson Jeffers: Fragments of an Older Fury (1968)
Archetype West: The Pacific Coast as a Literary Region (1976)

WILLIAM EVERSON

THE
MASKS
OF
DROUGHT

BLACK
SPARROW
PRESS
Santa Barbara
1980

ACKNOWLEDGEMENT

Some of these poems appear by courtesy of the following periodicals and publishers who originally issued them: *Ark*, *Brahma*, *Beyond Baroque 792*, *Choice*, Kingfisher Press, *Kyack*, Lord John Press, *Quarry*, Santa Susana Press, *Sequoia* and *Sierra Journal*.

LIBRARY OF CONGRESS CATALOGING IN PUBLICATION DATA

Everson, William, 1912-
  The masks of drought, poems 1972-1979.

  I. Title.
PS3509.V65M37   811'.52   79-93226
ISBN 0-87685-435-8
ISBN 0-87685-434-X pbk.
ISBN 0-87685-436-6 lim. signed ed.

To Susanna and Jude

TABLE OF CONTENTS

Storm-Surge 11

Goshawk 13

Runoff 15

Blackbird Sundown 17

Jay Breed 19

Steelhead 25

Cutting the Firebreak 29

Rattlesnake August 31

Chainsaw 35

The Visitation 45

Kingfisher Flat 49

Bride of the Bear 53

Moongate 57

Buck Fever 65

The Summer of Fire 71

Spotfire 77

The High Embrace 83

Stone Face Falls 87

Spikehorn 91

The Masks of Drought

Storm-Surge

Christmas Eve, night of nights, and Big Creek
Is on the move. At the equinox
Tempting rains toyed with us, teasing, and offshore at sea,
Beyond the slant sandbar blocking the rivermouth,
The great grey salmon skulked in the trough, dreaming the long
Genetic dream, plasmatic slumber of the unfulfilled,
Awaiting the moment of the forth-showing,
The river-tongue in the sea's vulva,
The strength in the slot.

            First incremental showers
Flushed dead vegetation, cathartic,
Purging the veins of the cleft mountain.
Then a month of drought reimposed itself,
The turbid summer's condign sterility
Drying the glades, sucking the flow back into the hills,
As if the mountain begrudged what it gave, called back its gifts,
Summoning them home, the high largess
Repentant of its grace.

            Advent broke dry,
December harsh on the hills, no sign of cloud
On the steely horizon. But solstice
Brought respite: a northwest flurry
Shook the last limbs bare, the drum of hailstones
Rattling the shingles under riddled cloud.
Then wind swung south and the nimbus struck,
One thousand-mile storm enveloping the coast,

Forty-eight hours of vertical rain, water falling
Like the splurge of God, the squandering of heaven—
As if forever on the mountains and the draws,
As if forever on the river-forks and creeks,
As if forever on the vast watershed, its sheer
Declivities, its seaward-pitching slides,
Thirst-shrunken slopes of the parched ridges.

And I lean in the dark, the harsh
Pulsation of night, Big Creek
Gorged in torrent, hearing its logs
Hit those boulders, chute that flood,
Batter their weight to the sandbar
And the sea, ripping a channel
Out to the future, the space beyond time,
On the eve of the coming, when Christ,
The principle in the purpose,
Splits the womb in his shudder of birth.

Goshawk

A rush of wings: the sound of sheer
Knife-thrusts, or the hatchet-stroke
Of thrown blades. Then the sharp
Slap, high up, a hurtling shape
Hitting thick branches. The great goshawk,
Knocked out of the sky, awkwardly teeters,
Clutching at twigs. But our canyon redtails,
His fierce tormentors, close in on him,
Snarling like cats. The stunned intruder
Takes off, uncertainly gliding. His pursuers,
Like vengeful priests, follow him out. Abruptly
The canyon is quiet. The morning sunlight
Calmly descends. The clean day
Soars on.

      What portent?

               Over the horizon
Some dark approacher forecasting his presence?
Or a movement out there from the larger life,
The nation, or the world? Or maybe
My own dark thought, a sudden impulsion of spirit
Momently intruding, to be harried forth,
Unable to challenge set purpose?
Or something more somberly glutted?
Some reflex of the life-force
Inconsonant with the whole,

And hence obtrusive, and unavailing?

Any or all. One waits to know.

But something was meant. In the visionary dream
A movement from beyond of the cosmic whole
Was registered here. In the wing-clash and the snarling beaks
A counter-force challenged the fixed field. But to no avail.
Met and overcome it was swept from consequence,
Evicted, thrown shuddering out.

Runoff

Four wet winters and now the dry.
All the long season a sterile frost
Grips the mountain, the coast like flanged metal
Bent thwart the sea. Above:
Stripped trees, taut-twisted branches
Catch stark white light. Below:
Shriveled creekbeds, raw to the air, run naked roots,
Obscenely groined through flaking rock,
The scat of torrents.

            Then early last evening
A thin drizzle, gaining toward dusk. Before dark dropped
The low-hanging cloud slit its belly and the rain plunged.
All night long the thirsty slopes drank straight-falling water,
Soaking it up, filling those tilted, deep-shelving seams,
Blue veins of the mountain, zig-zag crevices of fractured shale.
When dawn flared and the rain held
The runoff began.

            We rise with the light,
Sally down to the stream to touch fresh water
For a kind of blessing. We find instead a river of ink.
All the hoard of tributary creeks, those catchers of leaf-drift—
The strip of alder and the slough of fir,
Acrid shuff of the leathery tan-oak; and laurel,
The redolent, littering leaves of the laurel—
All that autumn-spun opulence
Frost drove down and ruthlessly squandered
Four moons back, to rot where it fell,

Now crawls to the sea, a liquid bile.

You look up at last in a wondering way
And exclaim softly, "Why, the mountain is menstruating!"
Something in your voice, a tremor there,
Tells of the mutual womanly pulse, the deep sensing,
Its sympathetic pang, its soft vibration.

Looking, I see indeed it is true:
Leaves like dead cells
Long held back in the frigid womb
Begin now to flow—under the rain
A deep cleansing, this rite of renewal.

For me it is runoff but my heart purges.

Touching you and creek-throb in the same impulse
I am healed of frost:
Woman and water in the blood-flow.

Blackbird Sundown

High Ridge Ranch: back of the barn
A live-oak thicket, and redwing blackbirds
In the late afternoon. They cluster on fence posts,
Twig stems, barbed wire, telephone lines,
Any proximate perch. Their brilliant epaulets
Gleam in the fading light,
Vivid scarlet on glistening black.
Intensely alive they frolic and strut,
Chatter the twanging blackbird tongue,
Jubilant in the bird-loud evening.

A sudden hush. In the suspension of sound
Silence drops to stunned terror.
Then all explodes, every bird for itself,
Up, down, out and away.

                For over the ridge,
Her shoulders of flight massively outstretched,
Her hunched body tense with hunger, gravid with need,
The Great Horned Owl glides implacably in,
Wide staring eyes fixed on her prey.

Instantly every bird recovers. Springing back to the defense
They converge on her, a racket of protest, a squall of imprecation.

Undeterred, she spans the yard, plunges into the oak thicket.
Behind her swarm the defenders, the stiletto beaks
Stabbing and yanking, a flurry of snatched feathers
Ragging her sides.

In a trice she emerges,
A half-dead fledgling gripped in each fist,
Her malignant face swinging right and left
As she scans the yard, glaring down her confronters.

Again the redwings close on her, railing and scolding,
Their punishing beaks a fury of reprisal.

She shrugs them aside, contemptuously,
And pauses a moment—ugly, umbrageous, triumphant.
Then she takes off, her dread profile
Humped in departure. Insolently unhurried
She clears the corral, skims the fence, and is gone.

And with her going the dusk drops. Where a moment before
Late light glimmered, now darkness
Swoops on the land.

The redwings
Circle and descend, seeking their roosts,
Pulling their shattered world back together,
Settling into the oak thicket, drifting toward sleep.

Out in the woods the she-owl's mate
Hoots once, hoots twice, his soft tattoo
Muffling the hush. She does not reply.
Her silence is the answer of the hearkening dead,
Listening for life, when life is no more.
Over the ridge the darkness shuts like a wing;
The earth-chill tightens; the claw moon
Talons the west.

Jay Breed

All the young summer the jay breed prospered.
The new brood, fledged early and growing apace,
Took over the canyon, a stellar triumph.
Bright, black-crested, sporting the razor-sharp profile,
They probed every cranny. Whatever accosted
Must pass inspection else suffer abuse.
Scolding, truculent, cunning, vindictive,
They strutted about the canyon, and we endured them.
Downstream by the meadow our creekside neighbors
Shot them with guns, then hung the skewed bodies in the apple
    trees
To scare off robbers. Here, under the towering
Canopy of redwoods, we let them live
And suffer their gall.

            And indeed their very abrasion
Bespeaks them: after the gloomy tree-sodden winter
That jaybird bravura fills a definite need.

I have, in fact, gone so far in complicity
As to scatter crumbs on an old stump to lure them in,
Swooping, blue iridescent streaks,
Angling through slant shafts of the sun
Between columned redwoods, their raucous bravado
My guiltful delight.

            But the cats
Are not amused. Skulking the yard they endure that umbrage
Nastily. Dive-bombed from behind
They crouch flat-eared and bare their fangs.

Often they scan the sky, the trees, the hedging thickets,
Possessed of a throttled rage, a passion
Apparently hopeless, given the jays'
Treetop immunity, but nursed nonetheless,
Corrosive desire clenched to the heart
Against the long-deferred accounting, the Great Day
Of feline retribution.

                    Meantime,
The jays cursed back, and streaked in,
Jeering.

              Then early afternoon,
The hour lazy and bland, a stripling jay
Dropped down from the trees to pick off a cricket.
At ease in the grass, confident of his long legs
For quick takeoff, he speared his game
With nice precision. Foiled in his beak
The hapless insect wriggled and strove.
Intrigued, the jay let it squirm,
Then flipped it aside, pounced, stabbed twice,
Artfully toying.

              But all unnoticed
In the wide summer day the black tom
Got his wits together. Aslink under the hibachi stand
He inched stealthily forward, tail twitching.
Suddenly the jay sensed him: one electric spring of those long legs
And he lit out, the cricket still foiling his beak.
Too late. Too late. Lightning unleashed, the black tom caught him
Full stretch in the rush, a foot off the ground and going away.
One terrified squawk sent the cricket spinning,
And bird and cat hit the grass together, a feathery tussle:

The end, the mad scrambling end and the clutched triumph,
Abrupt close of the long life-gamble.

                              Not yet. Not yet.

Pressed under the paws the jay's head struggled out,
Screeching piteously. The jay breed responded.
Converging from thicket and scrub,
From the tall stands of redwood and the streamside alders,
They closed in. The long flight-angles
Planed down, not jockeying now for scattered crumbs
But swooping for life, the only life they know:
The perdurable breed.

                    Wheeling above the crouched pair
They danced like blue devils.
The black tom grinned up at them,
His neck craned, his white teeth
Gleaming behind stretched lips,
His eyes yellow fire. Under his feet
The caught prey implored, piteously, the long lament,
The life-going.

              That hullabaloo
Brought the cat tribe in from the listening woods.
First little Squeak, least of the litter,
Who snatched the prey from her brother's paws
Distracted by jaybirds. But she, too, dawdled,
She, too, toyed with that pleading life,
Till her bigger sister, greedy minx,
Snatched it away, and with one clench of her jaw
Crushed the black-crested head.

Instantly all fell still, the fierce clamor hushed,
The yard deeply silent. From twig and branch the jays looked
    down,
Stunned, shaken. Then the parent bird
Gave the sharp *tut-tut,* abrupt signal of termination,
And they all took off.

            The cats
Ignored what they caught, left the futile remains,
Small wing-flurry of the spent cyclone,
Scattered in the grass. As for me,
Something within was held suspended,
The extravagant episode suddenly quenched,
Like a drench of ether splashed on my heart.
I picked up the disheveled, resplendent wings,
And stretched them to let the light fall through,
Translucent blue in the wild feathers. Then the arrogant tail
That had flirted with death and not won.
And for final gesture the elegant claw
Crooked at the sky.

            I took the numinous trophies
Inside the house to dry on a ledge. Well-placed,
Their iridescent message glows in the room,
To reveal from beyond the screen of Nature
The life of God.

            But what was the vibration
That trailed through the rooms as I bore them in,
And clings yet to my hands, like mountain misery?
A speck of blood flecked my fingernail.
Tasting, I imagined it salt.

But the moment was no more.

Outside, in the languid day, the black tom
Slunk beneath the hibachi stand and took up his post.
A touch of swagger, transmitted out of the fetch of the jay,
Invested his movements with auspicious pomp.
Oh, what animal cunning licked the feline lips,
Appeasement clean as a wing-bone whistle?
Reality reduced to a feather in the grass,
A plume in the fern?

Whatever death is
The jaybird learned it. But the black tom
Demurs, coiled in contradiction, the infinite
Satisfaction of life. Crouched on sheathed paws
He watches. His yellow eyes, blank as the sun,
Ceaselessly scan the jayless sky,
And not blink.

Steelhead

Incipient summer, scorch of the sun,
And the great steelhead shows up in our creek.
He lies in a pool, the shallow basin of a thin rock weir,
Impassively waiting. Ten days go by
And still he lingers. His presence
Is inscrutable. No one around here
Recalls such a thing: steelhead
Landlocked in summer.

                For the tag-end of April
Sees the last of them. Unlike all salmon,
Rising in winter to die at the spawn,
Steelhead commonly wrig back to sea,
Reclimbing the river-path year after year:
Continuous the trek, the journey joined;
Indomitable the will, the life-thrust.

But this? this aberration?
What is its meaning, and why here?
Deeper hideouts, below and above,
Where salmon and steelhead alike at the spawn
Await their time—those same deep holes
Are perfect places to bide out the drought
Were such his purpose. But no. Dangerously exposed,
In window-pane water he lies alone,
And waits. Inexplicably waits.

Dreaming last night I stiffly arose,
Groped my way down through scarred slopes
To a shallow pool. I knew it for his.

The moon, gibbous, lacked light to see by,
But sensing him there I made vaguely out,
Alone on the bottom like a sunken stick—
No, like a God-stoned monk prostrate in his cell—
That enigmatic shape, sleeplessly intent.
Daunted, I left him alone in that hapless place
And crept back to bed.

              To go down in the dawn,
Seeking him out as in my dream,
Holding him there in my mind's eye,
Still pointed upstream, smelling the high
Headwaters, while all about him
The dance of life sweeps rapturously on—

Giddy with delight the moths fly double.
In a spasm of joy the mayflies breed.
Above on the bank our Labrador bitch,
Massively in heat, hears her elkhound lover
Yelp on the hill and will not heel;
While under the weir the phlegmatic crayfish,
Gnome of these waters, ponderously grapples his viscid consort,
All fever aslake . . .

        Only myself,
Stooping to fathom his meaning here,
Know the tightening nerves . . .

              What his time portends
I dare not guess. But much or little,
Brief or prolonged, in this recondite presence
I am favored in my life—honored in my being,
Illumined in my fate. As hieratic gesture

He sounds the death-pang of abnegation,
Witness to the world.

　　　　　　Segregate,
Wrenched out of context, bearing the suppressed
Restlessness of all disjunction, subsumed
In the abstract dimension this bloodlife abhors—
Out of time, out of season,
Out of place and out of purpose—
Ineluctable pariah, he burns in my dream
And calls me from sleep.

　　　　　　Who am hardly surprised
To find by the water his scattered remains
Where the racoons flung him: tore gill from fin,
Devoured the life-sustaining flesh, and left in clay
The faint skeletal imprint—as fossil
Etched in stone spans time like myth—
The glyph of God.

Cutting the Firebreak

Mowing the east field under the ridge
I wade the wind. The bent-rib scythe found rusting in the barn
Swings in the sun; the ancient blade of my wife's great-grand-
    father,
Drawn from the dust of seventy years, riots in the grass.

"They don't make 'em like this old gull anymore!" cackled the
    smith,
Hunched above his spectral grindstone,
Shouting across the howl of iron and the fleer of sparks.
He paused, spat on the blade, wiping off rust. In the sudden silence
The wedding band he wore on his finger chimed fine steel.
Cocking his head like a listening bird he snatched up a file
    and rapped again.
"Hear that hum in her spine, that tone when she shivers?"
He barked harsh laughter. "Old timers
Got a name for it." Turning, he cut the power,
Stepped down from the bench. *They call it*
The moan of death!"

       And that hunger
Vibrates up the crooked stock as the grass reels.
I feel it hum in my arms; stroke on stroke
It sings in my shoulders; my collarbone
Rings to the pulse of it, the ravenous steel;
And I swing with it, made one with it,
Wheeling among the standing fern, goat-footed,
Trampling tall bracken, ruthless, the radiant flowers:
Iris, wild orchid, leopard lily—
The flush and shimmering splendor of life!

29

And then the honing: whetstone and steel
Kiss each other, they crave it so.
They lick their lips greedily together,
Like reckless lovers, or as the whore mouths the man.
I have to pull them apart.

The mad scythe

Hisses in the vetch, a snake denied, moans in the yarrow.
Whumph! Whumph! Oh, the grunt of lovers biting each other,
Stroke on stroke coupling through hell. It makes the sex
Growl in my groin to call them down, wild iris, lily,
The moan and the shudder. All the women in my life
Sprawled in the weeds—drunk in death.

Rattlesnake August

A rainless winter; week on week sun edging the hills,
And the frost's grey grip.

     Summer broke dry,
A tightness of heat clenched the sterile coast, a fierce parching.
No fog fended the light; a threat of fire
Stung the rustling air. By midsummer's moon
Leaves littered raw earth.

     Then late one dusk
Our Labrador bitch slogged home half lame,
Bleeding a little under the jaw, but we thought nothing of it:
Likely stuck on a thorn.

     Morning found her prostrate,
The head hugely swollen, the throat hemorrhaging blood.
"Snakebite," said the vet, "and she's too far gone.
Tonight she will die."

     We stared at each other.
Rattlesnakes in Big Creek canyon? Unheard of.
But the vet shook his head. "This God damned drought
Forces them down from their mountain dens
To creek water. We've known places this year
No snake's ever been seen in before,
And we're not done yet."

     Now, with night dropping,
We sit in the hot unnatural silence,
Awaiting the friendly scratch at the door

We know will not come. This loss is a wound,
Tearing the sensitive fabric of our life, and it aches in us.
We think of the snake out there in the dark,
Lurking, the vibration of evil,
Coiling under the roots of trees,
Alive beneath stones, listening.

I see tears blind your eyes.
Tonight, I know, you will tear my snake-totem
Down from the wall, and burn it, bitterly,
Your lips moving, your eyes blue ice.

I do not begrudge it: your way is best.

For two themes contend here: the loss and the menace,
Double pang of the twisted heart.
We braced for disaster, a vast conflagration,
A holocaust borne on an eastern draft sweeping down to the sea,
Burning homesites and bridges, driving the coastal population
Out onto the roads.

        It has yet to happen.
Rather, this subtle insinuation,
Gliding secretly into the warm nest
To spit venom.

        Because sunspots
Distantly flare on the fountain of fire
Must something displace, hit at man's life,
Take his friend and companion?
Whatever he loves, be taken, must go?

I leave the table, step out under stars,
Smelling dryness in the air. And death,
The presence of death.

                              Lurker in the dark,
Where are you?

                      Harried by heat,
Possessed of a taut desperation, the serpentine itch,
Driven down from some cool commodious hole higher up,
He descends, seeking water, water,
Raw slake for his thirst.

For he, too, loves life. He, too,
Craves comfort, smells it cunningly
Out. And when Fate accosts—
Licks his lip and stabs back.

Chainsaw

Three alders, shimmering
Graceful presences,
Swaying below the creek-bank,
Halfway down.

They will make welcome wood
Come winter.

I bring the blade,
Wiping it,
Handling it gingerly.

Scythes and axes I understand,
But the chainsaw?
What governs it?

The mechanistic fury.
The annihilate god.

I hear him moaning there,
Drawing the lovely alders down,
Calling them.

I feel the hunger of death
Pulse in his loins,
Tremble in his thews.

I smell his breath.

*

Settling the squat
Metallic beast on the ground
I grip the starter,
Spin once, spin twice.

With a deafening blast
The engine grabs,
Coughs, grabs again,
Then settles into it,
A rapacious snore.

Holding it forth in tense hands
I approach the trees,
Footing my way through vine-tangle,
Cautiously stepping.

As I move, the lethal snout
Roves ahead,
Snuffling for prey.

I place the blade,
Toothing the woman-smooth bark,
The naked skin.

My trigger finger crooks
And the chain leaps forward,
Chews white flesh.

Sawdust pours at my feet,
Spurts from the jagged gash like gore,
Like flowing blood.

*

Cutting in close
I lean on the steel,
The blade whining.

The tree starts over,
Then hangs there,
Hovering on its axis,
Death in its veins.

An ominous rushing of wind overhead,
A splintering shriek.

I scramble aside,
Watching it topple.
With a shattering crash
It hits, the heaviness
Flattening the air.

Fulcrumed across the granite lip
It twists crazily,
Butt flopping skyward.

I stand there staring,
The hushed saw whispering in my hands,
Asking, asking.

*

Next, number two.
Sheared through the trunk
It drops without a hitch:
A pushover.

Confident now I turn to the third.
The shrill saw whines,
Steel teeth tearing.

I bear down on it,
Forcing it, the blade
Snarling.

At last it goes over.

But as it crashes across,
Skinning the others,
The butt whips wide,
Spins toward me.

Startled, I step back,
One half-step back into—
Nothing.

Saving myself
I lunge forward,
A bid for balance,
But the blade stoops.

Suddenly I feel a terrible
Insinuative plucking at my knee,
A picking at my flesh.

It is the chain,
The chipping incisors,
The nipping teeth.

Just over my leg the lewd thing hovers,
Floating there, all its passion
Suspended in check,
Eager to pounce.

Appalled, I heave the beast up,
Falling back,
The blade rearing.

I hurl it aside and go down.

It lands on granite,
The chain spewing sparks,
The engine chattering.

Flat on my back
I struggle up and crawl over.
I cut the switch.

Then I look down.

     *

In a crystalline terror
I see the nick of shark-teeth
Etched across my knee:

The dreadful angle
On the blue denim,
The white-plucked thread.

Stunned, I pull up my jeans,
Looking for blood,
The target area.

Bald kneecap.
Naked thigh.

Not a scratch.

A gasp of relief
Delivers me.
Then a dizzying faintness,
Something clutching my throat.

Shaken, I get to my feet,
Leave the beast where it lies,
And hobble home.

Pouring myself a stiff one
I belt it down raw.

The slug hits like a fist.

In the still afternoon
I hear the shivering glass
Chip my teeth.

*

All evening long,
Musing alone,
The family away,
The house empty,

I sip my whiskey,
And feel for it,
The lopped leg:

Groping for something no longer there,
Something gone.

All evening long and the long next day
I hobble about on my pitiful stump.

Something is finished,
Something cleanly done.

Sprawled on the creekbank
The trees lie untouched;
I have no appetite for the saw.

I might have died there under those alders,
Bled to death before help came.

But that is not in the mind.

What is there is an absence,
A simple loss,
The lack of a leg.

Perfectly sound I hobble about,
Not the ghost of a member
Swung from my hip.

Not even a peg.

        *

And I think of the three graves,
Silent under hanging moss,
Up Scott Creek canyon.

Three clearly marked graves,
All pioneer women,
Peaceful in the sun.

But among them,
According to legend,
A man's leg is buried,

Torn off long ago by a sow grizzly
Protecting her cubs,
Then solemnly interred
In the quaint pioneer fashion.

Dust and ashes
The maimed member reposes.
But in my mind's eye
It glows in the ground,
Inseminating the female presences,
Instinct with seed.

Like Osiris, his phallus
Potent in death,
Or song-struck Orpheus,
Fragmented under the female fury,
The singing flesh.

And, musing, I let my fingers
Grope down, feeling,
Fumbling,

     Seeking
For what is no longer there.
Only the absence.

Only the emptiness,
The blank truncation.

The folly of the three alders.
The terrible stump.

The Visitation

Midsummer hush: warm light, inert windless air
Smoothing for sundown. We linger at table, sip wine,
Idly talking, the casual things of the day's dimension,
Our thought settling toward dusk.

                              Suddenly, in the vast
Calm of the canyon, an ominous crack, a break and snapping.
We look up alarmed. Something in the sound
Wrings our senses, flings us to our feet,
Slamming back chairs.

                        Then the crackling
Begins to rip, something going down out there
Tearing its guts out in an awful fall,
The air slashed by the shrieked agony of a form
Hauled down out of life, the shrill
Maniacal whine of fibers at last letting go,
The whoosh of a great weight falling, twisting as it drops,
Plunging toward chaos.

                        And then the crash,
The clobbering smash of that force as it hits,
The boom sweeping over like dynamite blast.
We gaze at each other, thunderstruck,
Utterly aghast—what in God's name!—
The terrible question in each other's eyes,
What skeletons toppling out of what
Unacknowledged closets, nakedly asprawl—

And then the aftermath,
Shock and counter-shock, agonized limbs

Snapping and thrashing, severance in the air,
Gash, splinter, rupture and slump. We hear lesser shapes
Taken down with it, hideously atwist, topple across.
We burst out the door, echoes pounding around us,
And dash down the road toward the wallowing sound,
Incredulous, stumbling and staring bewilderedly about.

For everything is changed. In the smash of disaster
Nothing looks the same, in fact is unseen—
The most familiar objects, house, trees, rocks, path,
All somehow displaced by the intrusion of violence,
The wretched dimension thrown over them all.

A hundred and fifty yards downstream
A wall of dust, like burnt gunpowder,
Yellow and angry, is boiling toward us.
Then, before it arrives, some last hanging branch,
Scraped off and hung up in the weight of passage,
Sickeningly lets go, a terrible finale.
The crack as it hits is a man's
Decapitated head dropped over a cliff:
We hear it thud and lie still.
Then a terrible silence floods back and engulfs us.
We wade through dust to that stunned place,
Expecting there we hardly know what.

A giant tree lies aslant the cut,
The narrowest part of the steep gorge,
Spanning creek and roadbed, a total block.
There it had stood, a great dead fir,
Daily passed by year in and year out,
But never seen, unnoticed in the dense foliage
Above and beyond us, where the road snaked by

46

Along the lightly-flowing creek
Through dense alder and laurel clumps,
Among strewn boulders.

Suddenly emerging,
Out of the long anonymity of its dream in the massed forest,
Expending its whole potential of life-force
In the apotheosis of its collapse, it staggers,
It descends.

You have in your mind the vision of this form
Secretly sprung from a blown seed
Three centuries ago, quietly growing unobserved,
Gaining tremendous girth and height,
Sucking sunlight above and water below,
Then slowly dying, to stand in death
Many decades more, until at last,
Having survived year after year the howling hurricanes
That whipped up the gorge, finally, in the utter
Calm of an August evening, suddenly letting go,
Pitching out of its ancient potential,
To shatter the canyon with its terrible scream,
Smash down the cliff,
Drop sharply across the shimmering creek,
Naked and fractured and stark,
A kind of final assertion of self,
The dropped trunk and branches
Blocking the trail. Nothing can pass now
Till chainsaw and peavey arrive and divide,
Section the torso, pull apart the limbs,
The crossed, sprawled members,
The fractured bones, and the crushed

Samson-like form of the prone giant.

Not Samson. A female thing, the high fork
Clearly denoting the vulva-crotch
Loggers call schoolmarms—
She lies sprawled and wanton in death,
Like a big-boned woman in a highway smash,
Half flung free, her twisted torso,
Laced with blood and lingerie,
Collapsed in the ditch.
Yokels arrive to stare dumbly down,
Brought dazedly out from their shattered supper,
But dare not touch . . .

                    Nor do we now.
We gaze and marvel. We stand in stunned silence.
We grope for words, twisting our anxious
Fingers together, talking low,
Letting our thoughts run on and on, aimlessly,
Till the drag of dark
Pulls over us, leaving between us
The shape of vast immensities, and above our heads
The stars' blunt dismissal.

Kingfisher Flat

A rustle of whispering wind over leaves,
Then the stillness closes: no creek-music,
No slurred water-sound. The starved stream
Edges its way through dead stones,
Noiseless in the night.

            I feel your body
Restless beside me. Your breathing checks
And then resumes, as in a moment of dream
The glimpsed image, mutely desired but scarcely believed,
Fades and revives.

           In the long drought
Impotence clutched on the veins of passion
Encircles our bed, a serpent of stone.
I sense the dearth in you also,
The bane that is somehow mine to impose
But yours to endure—cohibition of the blood,
Flaw of nature or defect of the soul—
Dry turning of leaves, cessation of desire,
Estrangement gripped in the roots of hair,
And around the loins, like a fine wire,
The cincture of nerves.

           I think of the Fisher King,
All his domain parched in a sterile fixation of purpose,
Clenched on the core of the burning question
Gone unasked.

           Out in the dark
The recumbent body of earth sleeps on,

Silent as dust, incognizant. Many a moon,
Many a withering month will she weary
Ere the black knight of storm whirls out of the West,
Churns from the turbulent fosse of the sea,
Assaults the shore, breaches the continental slope
And takes her, his torrential force
Stripping the iron zone of chastity
Down from her thighs, drenching belly and breasts,
All the pores of her famished body
Agape—

       Oh, wife and companion!
The ancient taboo hangs over us,
A long suspension tightens its grip
On the seed of my passion and the flower of your hope.
Masks of drought deceive us. An inexorable forbearance
Falsifies the face of things, and makes inflexible
The flow of this life, the movement of this love.
What prohibitive code stiffens the countenance,
Constricts the heart? What fear constrains it?
And whose the blame?

       Enough.
There is no need now, nor ever was,
For the ghastly rote of self-accusation
Scrupulosity enjoins. To find a new mate
Were nothing difficult for one so young, so lovely.

But something other, more inscrutably present,
Obtains here, possessing us, cohesive in spirit,
Divisive in the flesh—the lordly phallus
Never again to joust in the festive lists of love,
Quench its ardour in the uterine fens,

Assuage your cry?

Myth and dream
Merge in a consanguinity of kind,
Fuse the soul's wild wish and the hunger of the race
On the body's pang.

But something forbears.
Like Merlin and Niniane, bound in a fatefulness
That set them aside, wisdom and delight
Crucified in bed, polarized on the stretched extreme
That made them one, we twist our grievous fingers together
And stare in the dark.

I hear quaking grass
Shiver under the windowsill, and out along the road
The ripe mallow and the wild oat
Rustle in the wind. Deeper than the strict
Interdiction of denial or the serpentine coiling of time,
Woman and earth lie sunk in sleep, unsatisfied.
Each holds that bruise to her heart like a stone
And aches for rain.

Bride of the Bear

We camp by a stream among rugged stumps
In logged-over country. No tree shelters our bed.
In the year-long drought gripping the Sierras
There is now no snow, and the night is warm.
After our fog-haunted coast the air at this height
Seems weightless, without substance, almost clairvoyant.
Luminous stars, low overhead, look into our lives.
At ground level the campfire
Dapples the stumps, throws fitful shadows,
Guttering the dark.

              We drink late wine.
Arriving at dusk we had pitched camp quickly,
Eaten nervous supper. For a ranger going out
Warned of bear sign, and a wrangler behind him
Showed packs ripped open, bacon gorged. Seeing it
We prudently stashed our food in the jeep,
Gathered firewood, branch and root,
And built up the blaze. Fumbling through our gear
My hand touched in passing the great bearskin
Carried in from the coast, belated wedding gift
Brought along to delight you, a savage pelt to throw down by the
    fire,
Barbaric trophy in a mountain lair—but here,
In the actual presence, in bear country,
Furtively concealed: discreet hibernation
In the cave of the car.

              When the blaze dies down
I step out of its circle to fetch more wood

Against the presences of night. Standing in the dark
I look wondering up at those luminous orbs,
Hovering like moths just out of reach, preternaturally intense.
I sense around me the ghosts of slain trees,
Nude giants, slaughtered under the axe,
Pitching down from the slopes, the prone torsos
Hauled out with engines. Listening, I hear the famished creek
Drain west, a gurgle in a gravel throat,
Gasping.

       Back by the fire
You have fallen asleep, dazed with wine,
Curled by bright embers on living fern.
I lace a clutch of twigs on the coals
And in the spurt of flame see gooseflesh
Stipple your arm. Under the mellowing influence of wine
My nerves loosen, and I dismiss caution.
I fetch from the jeep the great bearskin
And draw it across you, then fondly step back to admire my care.
But what have I wrought that my own hand shaped
Yet could not forestall? Oh, most inadvertently
I have folded you in the bear's huge embrace,
A hulking lover, the brute body enveloping you,
Massively yours.

         You snuggle happily under it, sighing a bit,
The moan of a fretful satisfaction breathed from your deeps.
Is it wine on your lips that reddens them,
Or something deeper, in the bear's hug,
There, below the heart, a more elemental zone
At the body's base?

       I cannot tell.
But whatever it is it wantons your mouth,

And your mouth mocks me: inviting and denying,
The enigma of desire. I think, So be it.
Thus have I made you
Bride of the bear.

And thinking it,
The night chill shivers me, a sudden *frisson*,
The langour of wine possessing me.
I feel surge through my veins
The madcap days of our courtship,
Crazy monk and runaway girl,
Panting in discovery, goading each other on,
Wildly in love.

You stir in the bearskin.
Has memory touched you, two minds drenched in wine
Seeking each other through the cavern of sleep
Along the ancient line, the tendril of desire?

Drugged in dream you turn heavily. That nubile litheness
No longer is yours. But something better lives on in its place,
A mature abundance filling your flesh, the bloom of full life.

I, greybeard, nurse my drink and suck my pipe,
Watching the stars expire.

Now you turn,
Lifting your dream-drenched face to the light,
Still sunken in sleep, the wantonness
Splashed like wine on your parted lips.
Stiffly, raised on one elbow, you fumble at your blouse,
The heat under the animal pelt
Oppressing you. When your hand succeeds,

I see the naked globes of your breasts
Flash back the fire.

Bride of the bear.

Gazing up the dark I watch the stars
Cross the verge that shuts midnight from dawn
To walk down the west. Whatever happened to time?
When we pulled down our packs
The night lay before us. Now, in another hour,
Night is no more.

Somewhere out there
The ubiquitous beast, gorged on raw bacon,
Sleeps off his jag.

Raising your head
You look dazedly about, dimly comprehending,
Then sink back to sleep.

Around the campfire
The ghosts of slain trees look over us.
Out of the eastern peaks, traced now with light,
The dawn wind whispers. The starved stream
Gropes through the stumps.

Moongate

Las Gaviotas, Baja California

Something calls me from sleep.
I arise and go out, passing the bed
Where my brother and his wife,
Blanketed against the mild nightchill,
Lie side by side, at peace with themselves,
Serene in their world, the ineffable
Satisfaction of shared event,
The long-married.

        I recall how they met.
A young bachelor-foreman, out of sorts with himself,
He drifted about a vast city without direction,
Till an old craftsman on the job he managed
Admonished him:

        "Son, take my advice,
Don't live alone. Go to a small town,
Find the oldest girl of a large family,
And marry her."

        So it happened.
Thirty-nine years they have been together;
Their children are grown, their grandchildren
Half grown. I think of my own fragmented life,
Torn in two, the lost loves, the passions,
And wonder what karmic hazard
Promised the permanence
But denied me the term.

I open the door.
Standing on the threshold I gaze south and west,
Where the deep sky domes a wide bay,
Embracing the sea. The night is hushed,
The air winsome and smooth in balmy midsummer,
The vast sea dark, silent save for the abrupt thump,
An intermittent shuff of sudden wave,
Slapping the shore.

Glancing west,
I see the red moon low on the sea,
Sinking fast. A ribbon of cloud,
Sealing the horizon, divides like a curtain,
Closing a stage of consciousness,
Preparing for exit.

The moon hovers a moment.
It is nascently gibbous, two days past the half
In the waxing cycle, slightly misshapen, a youthful wife
Seductively pregnant.

I have not got a child.

Suddenly I sense my brother behind me,
Gazing outward across my shoulder.
"The Chinese," he whispers, "call it moongate,"
His voice kept low not to waken his wife.
Uncomprehending, I shake my head.
"The wake," he insists. "Look,
The path the moon makes there on the water."
Then I see it, a shimmering track,
Smoking on the swart sea's surface,
Reddishly gold, inviting and denying,

The way death does when it glints its promise
And withholds its peace.

My brother
Turns back to bed. Above the house
A flight of terns going west,
Invisibly talking together in the night,
Passes beyond, their strange speech falling softly about me,
The unearthly gutteral of an archaic tongue
Unknown to man.

And I think of Susanna,
Far to the north, deeply asleep in the redwood canyon,
Where the great horned owls
Chuckle together in thick-set darkness,
Hungry for quail.

And I remember again
Those madcap days and that courtship,
When we lay all night on the beach at Point Reyes,
Hearing surf shape the dunes,
While our souls, entranced, trod the moongate together,
Back down the path to man's beginnings,
That was yet our future.

How could we know what death it presaged,
That singleness of self at last given over,
The birth of new being?

The moon
Trembles a moment and then plunges in,
The suck of an utter surrendering,
Drawn to the depths of all beginnings,
The watery womb.

There is left only the night,
Stretched point to point of the dark horizon,
The night and the sea.

Bahía del Descanso,
Mexicans call it: "The Bay of Repose."

                                    Inside,
I hear the sigh of my brother's wife, turning,
Questioning and murmuring,
As he slips in beside her,
Settling to sleep.

Bahía del Descanso.
Something clutches my heart,
The sudden yearn of unrealization,
Where the moongate closed
And the nightbirds vanished.

A dream awaits me, back in bed,
And I turn to take it up.
Hovering on sleep I hear the ragged mutter of surf
Chewing the shore. The dawn wind
Rattles the blinds.

II

My brother and I are standing together
On the banks of a river. It is the Kings,
(Called *Rio de los Santos Reyes* by the Spanish)
Back in the country where we grew up,
Below Piedra (meaning *rock*) where the water
Pours from the mountains, flattens out on the plains.

It is springtime; grass is tall green,
And all about us the ubiquitous poppies
And wild purple lupine,
Pull in the wind.

On the slope above
Remnants of the old sugarpine flume
Lumbermen built to float logs from the mountains,
Still spans the gullies, skeletal remains,
Keeping tryst with time in these relic-less hills.

Not eighty years old, in so new a country
They yet embody the ineluctable past,
Residual traces of the ancient ones, the Pioneers, for us
As potent with meaning as Stonehenge,
And as evocative.

In the dream
My brother and I are high-school age
Or just past; but when I turn to speak
He is gone, following the river
Out onto the plains, off over the flatlands
To the cities of the world.

I myself
Turn back upstream, into the mountains.
They pile above me, ridge beyond ridge.
In the roots of my consciousness
They have always been there,
Aloof, majestic, their cloud-hung shoulders
And their imponderable brows,
Like congeries of ancestral fathers,

Gazing down on the distant breed they engendered,
And waiting, waiting . . .

                     Now Edwa is beside me,
My first love. The mountains are forgotten.
We go hand in hand, boy with girl
Through the magic springtime,
Rapturously in love.

               As if
All we will ever have is each other,
All we will ever need is each other,
All we will ever know is each other.

               As if
Nothing will ever exist but ourselves.

Suddenly, in peripheral vision,
I see the fox. He springs up before us,
Audaciously striking out to the left,
Looking back as he runs.

             The intrusion
Dazzles me. Edwa does not see him,
But tearing my gaze from her eyes as I turn,
I follow the fox.

            He leaps through the grass,
Dodging and twisting, half-crawling,
Then inexplicably showing himself,
Seductively beckoning, only to disappear again,
Running rapid as light.

                    Rust red,
Somehow flecked with blue, like fire,
And the flowing tail like a flame, he runs,
He beckons and runs.

                    Now Edwa is gone.
But still I press forward, urgently,
Following the fox, the illusive one,
Fleeing, beckoning.

                    Then I remember:
It is the great canyon of the Kings,
High in the mountains, the inaccessible
Headwaters, the abode of God.

To this am I drawn.

Now I hear someone running behind me.
Looking back I see her, the strange woman.
She is following, watchfully intent,
Not seeing the fox but sensing what I seek,
The mysterious bourn, the quest.

Returning to the trace
I press on up the river,
Following the fox.

When the dusk draws down
I look back at the woman.
As if by sign she moves up beside me.

What I follow she cannot see,
But what I see she follows.

And her eyes are shining, shining.

Buck Fever

Drought-stricken hills. Somewhere ahead
Lay a waterhole, and the thought
Moistened his mouth. But there was no game,
And late in the day, the camp calling him back,
He relented: "To hell with it. One more swing
Round this blistered ridge and I'll give it up."

Then deer-scat in the trail, buck shit
By the size of it, and, sure enough, there in the dust,
One fabulous print . . .

                    "Son of a bitch!"

A rustle of leaves in the scrub oak,
A thump of hooves on dry earth
Stopped him in his tracks.
Eyes fixed on that muffled ripple of sound
His pulse skipped, then pounded on.
Something cautiously moved there, that much was sure.
Then the great crowned head, the twelve-point antlers
Rode slowly across his line of vision
Between two trees, but instantly gone,
And the footfall checked.

                    The buck, warily upwind,
Had not caught his scent. He crept forward two steps
But his foot scuffed twigs and the beast snorted.
Suddenly it minced into view, nimbly,
On tiptoe, ears up, nostrils flared,

The arched neck craning—and the eyes,
The liquid eyes in the spade-shaped face,
Staring.

      He stood transfixed.
"Oh God and Jesus," his heart whispered,
Then his brain sang: *This is it!*

                But suddenly
A giant hand reached out of that presence and gripped him cold.
Something in the beast itself, motionless there,
Reached out of its magical shape and possessed him,
An invasion of awe.

        His arms shuddered,
Hands fluttering rags. The rifle, cantilevered ahead,
Wobbled between them. As he strove to raise it
An eternity of helplessness sucked down his strength,
Wrung him limp.

      Then, in a sudden convulsion,
His whole being revolted, cracked the somnambulism
Of desire that held him in thrall,
Shook him free.

      Pitching rifle to shoulder
He got off a shot, the report smashing the silence.
The buck jumped sideways, a shocked nerve,
As if the sound alone had struck it broadside
And thrown it back.

      Suddenly it broke,
Took one long incredible leap,

Spun away, cleared a fallen log,
And was off, a tawny streak.

With the back of his hand he kicked the lever,
Heard the fresh shell slam in the chamber.
Crash! His head jerked as if punched,
The gun muzzle whipping. He kicked shell after shell,
Crash! Crash! plugging the emptiness
Round the vanishing shape, a crazy staccato.
When the hammer snapped on blank steel
He dropped his arms, his retina
Retaining the futile spurt of gravel
His last shot picked on the shale slope
Above and behind the streaking shape
Before it was gone.

       He stared, disbelieving.
There was the jagged hole in space that had held it.
There was the magical moment, and the rent silence
That let it go. There was the acrid reek of gunsmoke
Stinging his nostrils.

       No more. Nothing more.

Looking about him, suddenly aware of the low fading light,
Everything burned pure: the squat trees,
The stiffly hunched hills, the bleak
Pitch of the sky.

       And the remoteness, the wrenched
Remoteness of it all.

       He sank down on a log,

But instantly climbed to his feet,
Seeking proof, the crucial verification,
The track of the buck.

When he found it
The clear etch of its print in the thin dust
Was the sign of a wonder his infancy knew,
But thought could not reach.

There was no blood.

He stood there a moment,
Letting the fever fade from his hands,
Fade from his knees and his fluttering heart.

When his nerves steadied
He shoved three cartridges into his gun,
But it took four.

Where the empty shells
Lay scattered about the print of his boots
He stared dumbly.

There were four, all right.

Picking them up
He tossed them pensively into the brush,
One by one, where none could be seen.

Then he went back.

That night in his dream
A puma stalked a dappled fawn under bristlecone scrub
But missed its quarry.

Next morning,
Sousing his face in mountain water,
Something he'd learned once long ago
Slid into his mind:

The fawn has no scent.

He thought of the hollow space,
The weird light that held the buck
Before it vanished, and a childish wish
Crossed his mind:

A silver bullet.
Fake out that magic.
Kill that devil.

Stooping to drink
He glimpsed his own furred face in the ripple,
Those strange eyes in the deep.

The Summer of Fire

"California is burning!" The voice of the newscaster,
Portentous and somber, tolls off a hundred spotfires
Strung up the State, from the South San Gabriels
To the Siskiyou chain.

                  Ten days back
Thunder rattled us out of the house at dawn
To scan the sky and watch dry lightning
Walk on the hills.

              Why the Santa Cruzes
Never caught fire no one could guess.

                        But eastward,
Across the inland oven of the Central Valley,
The entire Sierra felt the whiplash fall,
And in the withered tinder of a two-year drought
Canyons threw smoke like the belch of chimneys
Tonguing the sky.

              North of us
Mount Diablo wrapped itself in a crimson mantle
And claimed its name: a surging inferno.

                      To the south
Big Sur exploded: impacted brush,
Flattened by heavy snowfalls of the past, lay on the slopes,
Fifty tons to the acre round the Ventana Cones,
And the runaway burn tore rugged country
Like a raging bull.

71

This morning at dawn
The sun rose bloody through a pall of smoke
From sixty miles south. At noon
Our shadows, askew on the ground,
Cast an amber aura.

        It gives a weird refraction,
Something unspeakable, covertly glowering behind one's back,
Edging into view when crisis looms.

              I waggle my weight,
Make the aural demon dance, thinking,

                  "So?

The white light around the body
Turns angry when denied?"

          *

        Angry and umbrageous.
City people shake their heads and thank their stars
But the local folk are sardonic: they've been through it before.
When a young State Forester knocks at the door
And hands us a list of printed regulations:
Clear every building down to mineral soil sixteen feet back,
We thank him grimly and reach for our rakes.

But the widow McCrary, from the porch of the house in which
    she was born
Seventy years past, glances at the list
And glares at the man:

        "I resent this. Our people
Took care of this country before your department

72

Ever was dreamed of." The offending document
Flutters to the ground. "We don't have to be told what to do."

I stand in the dusk on Kingfisher Flat and think,
"How beautiful!"

        Pride, itself fiery, incites defiance,
Rising out of the char of the past
To re-envision crisis—what came as affliction
Lives on in the mind as a kind of grace,
Restored to legitimacy in the distancing of time,
Made memorable through struggle.

               And indeed
Out on the flat the twin giant redwoods
Carry the scars of ancient fire from centuries back,
Ennobling them, were that possible, with the dignity of pain.

Farther up the slope the blackened hollows of burnt-out stumps
Honor the primal war between them,
Vegetation and flame.

        One is life and one is death,
Yet polarity binds them. Definition is the clue.
Only out of the screaming tension, each true to its own,
Comes clarification.

        *

        Procreation and death.
The conflagration of sexuality
Whips through the taut congestion of nerves,
Like the van of fire in the canyon sluices,

Singeing and searing, scorching root and branch,
Tendril in the mesh, driving the beleaguered ego
Back and forth between the rages of excess.

A year of extremes. Creek-bottoms
Flake with the frosts of winter; flash floods shatter;
High ridges endure the fires of drought.
Season on season the great God of All Weathers
Grinds down the mountains, reducing the coast
Under the hands of those terrible abrasions,
While man, a pigmy, dances between them,
Dodging fire and water, reeling beneath the twin flagellations,
Shaking a puny fist at the sky, cursing and blaspheming,
Till old age chastens him to dignity at last.

And what of me? Has age brought peace?
Imposing a wry chastity
On the flammable mind?

                    To the contrary.
The pummel of suppressed exultance
Rages through me, crying,

                    "Burn! Burn!
All you dead grasses, fallen under the scythe,
Wild iris, leopard lily, sweep skyward in flame,
Meet fire in heaven with fire on earth!"

I look up above at the towering trees,
That took at the root the red demon
From time out of mind, monumentally impassive,
And I cry,

"Burn! Burn!
O chaste ones, magnificent presences,
Scream in the ecstasy of consummation,
Torch and expire!"

I gaze wildly about at the rim of the sky,
Craving a luridity of glare,
My eyes smarting, my nostrils
Flared.

Only the dark drops.

Inside the house my young wife
Fixes the supper, her lithe body
Moving between the table and the stove,
Sinuously alive.

I look at the sky
One final time. Over my head the first star
Glitters through haze, a liquid agate.

And I think: Whatever
Idiot catastrophe the heart craves,
This is the peace.

Let autumn
Bring in its wake what it will or can,
The summer is supreme.

Old earth
Hugs pure fire down deep at her heart,
And banks power.

Spotfire

A single cap pistol,
Found on a shelf in a local market,
Left over from the Fourth.

Bought with his carefully hoarded coin
It hangs in his hand,
Cradled home through the heat.

Whipped from the hip,
Snapped fast, multiple explosions
Shatter the calm, break
The lazy afternoon.

He cocks and fires,
Cocks and fires,
The solitary sport of the only-begotten.

Round the corner of the house
He twists and slithers,
Fleeing bandits,
Then down across the creek
And up the other side.

Behind a fallen log
He flops on his belly,
Himself now the bandit, picks off
The converging posse.

Plunging back to the creek,
Bullets zinging about his head,

He makes his getaway,
Disappears down the road.

        *

A half-hour later
I stand in the yard of Kingfisher Flat,
In the late light,
Barefooted, gazing leisurely about,
Smelling the air of approaching autumn,
The rare tang of fall,
Before drifting indoors
To mix the first drink.

Suddenly my eye, attracted upslope,
Catches color, a bright blaze,
Fire crackling up the skewed log.

                "What the hell . . . "

I grab up a bucket, yelling to my wife.
She comes out the back, wondering,
Sees fire sharp on the hill
And her face blanches.

I race for the creek,
Aghast, bucket in hand.
There is hardly water,
But somehow I scoop it,
Half a pail at best,
And climb the steep slope,
Twisting and slipping,
My feet bleeding.

Where an eight-year-old kid
Scampered like a chipmunk
I can hardly crawl.

Just in time I reach it,
The climbing fire,
And the water dashes it down.

Sliding back to the creek
I hit hard. My wife,
Standing slipper-deep in muck,
Hands another bucket,
Full and slopping over,
And I start the crawl back.

Now the boy shows up out of nowhere,
Running scared, grabbing pails,
Tin cans, fruit jars,
Anything to hold water.
Suddenly beside me,
He sloshes burning punk.

             Three trips and it's out,
             The blaze quenched.

We stand in the creek, the three of us,
Panting, thoroughly frightened,
Looking up at the hill,
The tangled thicket,
Mountain brush, tall standing timber,
Looking up the long half-mile of hillside above us,
And thinking:

Beyond it the range,
The crackling heat of fire-prone September,
And beyond that the State . . .

Incredulously staring, hardly daring to ponder
What a minute or two more
Must surely have meant.

(Who would have thought
The paper cap of a toy pistol
Could ignite the world?)

Breathing gratitude to God
For deliverance, the spared moment,
The sudden reprieve.

＊

Two days later the episode is fading,
But what is etched in my mind
Is the glob of fire in the late light,
Orange red, the flames licking up,
A burning core of intensity,
Like the essence of a giant fruit,
As if we were being shown,
Through a slit in the skin,
The fiery inside:
A hole in the surface
To another dimension—

As if suddenly
Through the film of the earth
A flame stuck out its tongue,

Licking greedily,
Exposing all the impacted fire
Compressed at its heart.

And I fix my sight on it, my eyeball
Glued to the glory hole of a blast furnace,
Shaken by the intensity within,
The terror, a fury
Utterly belied by the inert scruff,
The thick vegetation
Masking the hill.

It is crisis
Makes intensity intense.
Reality real.

Place consequence in the scales
And watch the pans shiver.

Put fire and death,
Guilt and mortality
In the obsessive choice
And feel the nerves tighten.

I have seen my heart's fate
Shaped in the balance,
And known what I am.

But does *he*?

His cap pistol
Is contraband till wet weather,
And he truly knows why.

But is knowing
Enough? Is knowing
Ever enough?

I look up above at what might have been,
What fate just missed,
Black char climbing the sky,
Ten thousand acres of smouldering ash.

Somewhere, in the interstices of the self,
Like molten lava at the earth's core,
The principle of existence
Possesses its essence,
Primal, dangerous, unpredictable.
Out of our wayward impulses
It flashes and breaks free.

And I whisper:

      Lord, may what has been learned
Be learned in depth.

      For him.
For me.

The High Embrace

They stand in the clearing of Kingfisher Flat,
Twin giants, *sequoia sempervirens,* the ever-vernal,
And take in the arms of their upper branches
The last light crossing the bench-ridge west,
Sinking toward dusk.

          Standing between them
I look up the double-columned space to the soaring crown,
Where those red-ribbed branches clasp each other in a high
    embrace.
For hundreds of years they have stood here, serenely apart,
Drinking clear creek water through sequaceous pores,
Feeling the flake of mountains sift chalkstone gravel about
    their boles,
Watching giant grizzlies scoop gravid salmon on the spawning
    bars below,
And tawny cougars stalk for fawns in their leaf-dappled shade.
They heard the kingfisher chirr his erratic intemperate cry,
While over their tops the slow-wheeling condors circled the sun,
Drifting south to their immemorial roosting ledges in the
    Los Padres peaks.
And they felt the demon of fire lick its running tongue up
    their shaggy skin
And not flinched, scorched but unscarred in the long warfare,
The stress-tension shaping fuel to fire,
The life-flux of their kind.

          Tonight,
In the heat of the drought, we will forsake our bed,
Shutting the house-presence out of our thought,

Taking our respite in the open air. We will muse late,
And lay ourselves down by fir-bark embers,
Under the cape of the twin redwoods, swept back in time
A thousand years when this coast nurtured its kind—
The great beasts, the towering trees, the bird-flight migrations,
The shy coastal tribes. And in the sea-troughs of sleep
Our dreams will mirror the world above
Where stars swim over, and shadow the bloodstream's sibilance,
All through the foliage of the flesh, its fern-like fronds.

Up there above me the last light
Filters in as through stained glass windows,
Diffuse, glowing in the lofts of the upper branches,
Radiant and soft. And the mystery of worship
Descends on me, out of those far fenestrations.
And the God-awe, wake-wonder, envelops me,
Between the monumental straightness of columns
Bearing the sky, illuminate zone, twin towers
Conjoined above, clasped in the high embrace,
The soaring arch.

                    And the face of my son
Dawns between the gigantic boles
As he runs to meet me. And I ask in my heart
The graciousness of God, that he may grow in their presence,
As the tan-oak grows, as the fir-tree and fern,
As the chipmunk and the jay shelter under their span.

And I invoke their mystery of survival,
That the lightning-shattering years,
And the raw surge of fire,
May skim but not scar him—
As they themselves are scathed but unscarred—

Through the skip years of his childhood
And the leap years of his youth.

Make over our heads, then, the high embrace,
Like a blessing, the numinous descent, faith-fall,
Out of the heights, the leaf-light canopy,
The lofts of God, induplicate,
A gift regiven, the boon bestowed.

Stone Face Falls

Sheer naked rock. From the high cliff-cut
Straight falling water. Caught halfway down in a stone socket
It checks, boils over, then widens as it drops,
Snaking dreamily into the rockpool below.
Many months back it roared in flood;
Now, in the grip of drought, Big Creek the brawler,
Tamed and gentled, takes this pitch like a gliding dancer,
A shimmering sleeve against dark waterstains,
Storm-trek of the past.

        We have come,
The two of us, in the white heat of noon,
To bathe at the fall-foot, a lambent pool
Under the salmon-stopping cliff.
We are struck by silence, the reduction of force,
Recalling those thunderous torrents of the past,
When the wild cataract drove everything before it,
Generating in its plunge a saturating gale,
Sopping a man a hundred feet below,
Drenched to the eyes in stinging spume.
But now, in the drought, the diaphanous film
Ripples down the rock, maidenly, a silken
Scarf, the veil of a bride, as virginal
And as lovely.

        Over our heads the great stone face
Juts from the gorge, a chief's visage hewn in raw granite,
Staring north, gazing down the long south-trek of his people,
Ten thousand years from the Bering Strait.
And the mystery keeps, the indomitable spirit

Guarding the secret where the water pulses,
The source, the slowed rhythm at the timeless center,
The heartbeat of earth.

I lower my gaze.
You are standing under the waterfall, nude, your body
An ivory wand against the seamed granite.
It is gleaming there, wreathed in water,
Breasts erect. The woman belly
And the female thighs
Shine in a shimmering ripple of lace,
The circling stream.

I move to meet you.

Suddenly a kingfisher swoops between.
In midflight he sees us, veers sharply,
Utters a sudden electrifying screech,
The ineluctable tension cruxed at the heart of things
Splitting his beak, the mystery
Out of which life springs and from which it passes.
Three times he circles, skirling his fierce
Importunate cry, then climbs the thermal,
The lazy updraft transcending the falls,
And disappears up the canyon.

You hold out your arms.

Dropping my clothes
I enter the pool,
Wade the ripple to where you stand.

It is the longest walk—
Out of the glacial

Past, through the pulsing present,
Into the clenched
Future—man to woman
Through time-dark waters.

                              Far ahead,
Beyond the stone face of the falls,
The cry of the kingfisher
Pierces the noon.

Spikehorn

The yearling buck, shot through the lungs,
Made it out of the brush and halfway to the stream
Before he fell. The illegal hunter
Never followed through. What dropped in the meadow
Died where it lay, unnoticed by any save two red bulls
Fenced in that field.

              The following day
A great black bird rose up when we came,
Lurched clumsily off, the wings made for soaring
Baffled now in this hemmed enclosure,
This deep forest field.

              Late that night
The coyotes found him. We heard from afar
The yelping chorus, clamoration of the feast,
High sung litany to the winnowing of time,
The brevity of life.

              Early next morning
The great bird was back with a dozen others,
A vulturine horde. Ghouls out of hell
They perched on the carcass, angling each other out
At the plucking, obscenely gobbling
The riddle of gut.

              Our abrupt arrival
Sent them hissing aloft to circle and alight,
Teetering and balancing on the tall fir tops,
Refusing to abrogate their ancient
Prerogative, their ancestral place
At the sharing of the kill.

Two days later
The sentinel bulls stood over the torn and scattered remains,
Bellowing, lugubriously lowing, solemnly lamenting
The passing away of all slotted-hooved kind,
Mourning the death of their nimbler comrade,
Little cousin of the woods.

We paused there,
Disbelieving, and spoke to them as best we could.
They stared back, uncomprehending, not to be consoled.
Chagrined, we trudged on.

The following weeks
Left nothing much but a chewn shinbone and a scrap of hide.
No birds in the sky, no movement in the woods.
Nothing but the sparse pasture, the two red bulls
Placidly cropping the lank cover,
An emptiness in the air.

Then the changing year
Brought a leaf-flurry. Equinoctial rains
Replenished the earth. In the body-print of the buck
The first green grass quickened the bronze.

And we said:
The cycle is complete,
The episode is over.

But the silence that hung about that place
Was haunted, the presence of something anciently ordained,
Where we, unwitting acolytes, with the birds and the bulls
Enacted its rite: there in the immemorial clearing,
The great listening mountain above for witness,
The sacrificial host between the river and the woods.

NOTE

Inspired by the unprecedented drought that gripped the West in 1976-77, I have departed from my usual practice of chronological arrangement, and have placed the poems in the line of seasonal progression.

In "Kingfisher Flat", perhaps the key poem of the series, the figures of Merlin and Niniane are of course drawn from Arthurian legend; but rather than following the version of Mallory (Merlin and Nimue) or that of Tennyson (Merlin and Vivian), both of which depict the sage ensorcelled by a vixen, I have utilized the reflections of Heinrich Zimmer in *The King and the Corpse*, who saw the pair in terms of the archetypal attraction between Wisdom and Folly, and so have retained the usage employed there.

W. E.

Printed January 1980 in Santa Barbara for
the Black Sparrow Press by Mackintosh & Young.
Design by Barbara Martin. This edition is
published in paper wrappers; there are 500
hardcover trade copies; 250 hardcover copies have
been numbered & signed by the author; & there
are 50 copies handbound in boards by Earle
Gray, each containing a holograph poem by
William Everson.

Photo: John Knight

Born in Sacramento, California, in 1912, William Everson has shaped his lifework into a sequential trilogy entitled *The Crooked Lines of God.* Thus his early San Joaquin Valley and World War II period, *The Residual Years: Poems 1934-1948* stands as natural thesis. Opposite it ranges the supernatural antithesis of *The Veritable Years: Poems 1949-1966,* tracing his Dominican decades as Brother Antoninus. Since then *The Integral Years: Poems 1966-* marks, as synthesis, his return to secular life. Within this movement *The Masks of Drought* constitutes a distinct advance.

Everson's honors include a Guggenheim Fellowship in 1949, a Pulitzer nomination in 1959, the Commonwealth Club of California's Silver Medal in 1967, the Shelley Memorial Award in 1978, and the Book of the Year Award of the Conference on Christianity and Literature, an affiliate of the Modern Language Association, also in 1978. Everson is presently Poet-in-Residence at Kresge College, the University of California, Santa Cruz.